THE
CHILDREN'S
BIBLE TREASURY

THE
CHILDREN'S
BIBLE TREASURY

Retold by Leonard Matthews

Contents

Published by Peter Haddock Limited,
Bridlington, England.
Courtesy of Martspress Limited. ©
Printed in Russia.

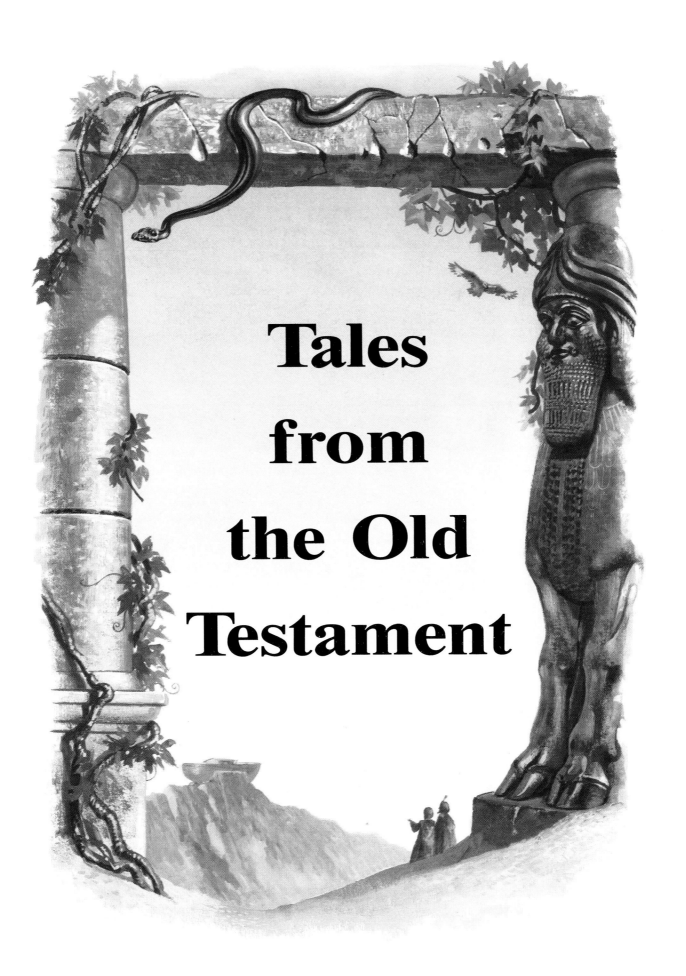

Tales
from
the Old
Testament

Noah and the Great Flood

A long, long time ago there lived a good man, named Noah, and his happy family. One day God spoke to Noah. "Ever since I made the world," said God, "the people have become more and more wicked. Today you and your family are the only really good people in the world. Now listen to what I say. The world will be covered in a great flood."

Poor Noah. How shocked he was. But God told Noah that he and his family would not be drowned. ''Build a great boat,'' said God. ''Then gather together all the animals in pairs, one male and one female, and take them and your family on board the boat.'' Noah obeyed God and no sooner had he and his family and all the animals boarded the boat than mighty storms broke out all over the world.

Inside the boat, which Noah called an ark, he and his large family closed all the doors and windows and huddled together. Lightning flashed and thunder crashed. For weeks the terrible storms went on and on and floods spread further and further over the world. At long last there was not another living thing to be seen above the water. As God had promised, the world had been flooded.

"Will these storms never cease?" wondered Noah sadly. "Our food is running short. Soon there will be none left and we will all starve." The storms *did* cease but the water continued to rise for a further one hundred and ten days. At last it began to recede. How Noah, his wife, his sons and daughters and his sons- and daughters-in-law thanked God. Now Noah had a pet raven. One day he set it free. It flew away and was soon out of sight. Noah waited but the bird never returned. Then Noah sent out a dove. Some time later it returned tired out. It had found no place to land. A week later Noah set the dove free again and the following day it came back.

This time the dove had a leafy twig in its beak. It had been plucked from an olive tree. At last Noah knew that the level of the water was falling. A few days later the ark jolted as it came to rest on the side of a mountain.

Joyfully, Noah and his family and all the animals left the ark. As they did so, they saw a rainbow in the sky. Then God spoke. "I will never again flood the earth," He said. "Rainbows will always remind you of my promise."

The Tower of Babel

Noah's sons and daughters were ordered by God to have many children. They did so and their children grew up and had more children. So the time came when there were many people on the earth again. They all lived in a place called Babel. But God wanted them to spread out and live all over His world. He ordered them to do so. "No," they replied. "We want to stay in Babel. We will make our city even bigger and we will build a tower so high its top will reach to heaven." God was angry. "So long as they have one language," He thought, "nothing will ever separate them." So He came down and made them forget their language.

They all began to talk strangely. It sounded nonsense. They laughed but could not understand each other.

Suddenly a fierce storm came and the frightened people ran here and there not knowing where they were going. They left their city and lived in different parts of the world. They spoke different languages. God had succeeded in His plan to spread mankind over all the world.

Abraham's Long Journey

This story is about one of the greatest men of the Bible. When he was born he was called Abram. Later, though, God changed his name to Abraham. Our story starts in the town of Haran where Abram, who was a rich man, lived with his wife, Sarai, and his young nephew, Lot.

Abram had many servants and shepherds, many flocks of sheep and many herds of cattle and camels.

One day God spoke to Abram. "You must leave Haran," said God, "and set out for a far land. I will guide you. There you and your people will build a mighty, new nation. I will take care of you."

Abram obeyed God and set out on his long journey with all that he owned. The journey lasted for many weeks. At last they reached a place called Bethel.

It was here that, unhappily, Abram's followers and Lot's followers started to quarrel and fight. Abram could see that there would be no end to the ill-feeling. He said to his nephew, "It would be wise, Lot, for us to part."

Lot agreed and, after a sad farewell, he and his followers set out to find a place where they could settle. He came to a place in the valley of Jordan called Sodom. It was a wicked city.

Meanwhile Abram and his family and followers settled in Bethel. They put up their tents and began to work hard, tilling the land, growing their crops and tending their animals. Years passed and all went well with Abram.

But in Sodom, Lot and his people found themselves in great danger.

There was a great King of Elam who was an enemy of Sodom. One day he decided to conquer the city. He gathered together a great and powerful army and with his mounted warriors close behind him he led them forth to battle.

The people who were living in Sodom were lazy and evil. They had become used to an easy life and it did not take long for the King of Elam and his powerful army to break through into the city and capture it. And all the people in Sodom were made prisoners.

The King of Elam and his army stole all the gold, jewels, money and cattle belonging to the people who lived in Sodom. Then they left the city and took the people with them to work as slaves. Lot and his family were amongst them. When Abram heard what had happened he called together an army of his own and set out to rescue Lot. He took the army of Elam by surprise, at night, defeated it and rescued Lot and his family. He left behind him only the fallen army of the King of Elam.

A Son for Abraham

Lot was delighted to be rescued. He and his wife and two daughters thanked Abram and went back to Sodom. Many years passed and Abram and his wife, Sarai, lived happily except for one sadness. They had no children. Then, one evening when Abram was out alone, he heard the voice of God.

"Do not be sad, Abram," said God. "Look around you. As far as you can see, this land belongs to you and your people. And one day you shall have a son. This I promise."

When Abram told Sarai what God had told him, she brought to him her young servant, Hagar. In those days men often married more than one wife. "Marry Hagar," Sarai told Abram. "Perhaps she will be the mother of your son." Sarai went on to tell Abram that she thought she would never have a son of her own. At last Abram agreed to marry Hagar. Then came the day when Hagar gave birth to a baby boy. Abram was happy as he held the baby but it made Sarai worried. She wondered if Hagar might become more important to Abram than she was.

"My son will be called Ishmael," said Abram. The name Ishmael means 'He Whom God Hears'. Abram was happier than he had been for many years.

Then, one day when Abram was out walking, God spoke to him again. Abram fell to the ground as God said, "From now on you are to be known as Abraham, 'The Father of Many'." God also told Abraham that Sarai should change her name to Sarah, which means 'princess'. "She will have a son," God said. "He will be the first of a mighty nation."

"But what of Ishmael?" asked Abraham for he loved Ishmael. "I have other plans for Ishmael," replied God.

Abraham wondered when all this would happen.

The Three Strangers

Then one day three strangers appeared outside Abraham's home. Abraham welcomed the three strangers and invited them to eat. One of the men who seemed to be the leader suddenly said, "Your wife, Sarah, shall have a son, Abraham." At once Abraham knew that the stranger must be God. He went on to tell Abraham that He knew his nephew, Lot, was living in Sodom.

"Abraham," God added angrily, "you should know that Sodom and Gomorrah are the most wicked cities on earth and I have made up my mind to destroy them."

Abraham pleaded with God not to attack Sodom. "My nephew and his family might die," cried Abraham.

After a while God nodded. "Very well, on one condition," He said. "If ten good people can be found in Sodom, I will not destroy it." Then God and the two men went on their way. The next day while Lot was sitting at the gate of Sodom, speaking with some friends, two men who were strangers approached.

Lot noticed that the men were very weary and kindly invited them to go home with him to rest and have something to eat. The men agreed and later told Lot that they were messengers from God.

"Yesterday we spoke with your uncle, Abraham," one said. "We are here to tell you, Lot, that tomorrow Sodom and Gomorrah will be destroyed." Lot believed the stranger and begged for his wife and two daughters to be spared.

"If we can find ten men in Sodom who are not wicked," the second stranger said, "the city will not be destroyed. You and your family, though, must leave Sodom early tomorrow morning. Now listen carefully. If you value your lives you will not turn to look back at the city when you leave." Then the two men went on their way.

Early the next morning Lot, his wife and their two daughters hurried out of Sodom.

Suddenly, from behind them, they heard a tremendous crash followed by a blinding light. Lot's wife turned her head toward Sodom.

Lot's wife had forgotten that God's messenger had warned that nobody was to look back.

Instantly she was turned into a pillar of salt. Lot and his daughters could only hurry away as fast as possible.

From far off Abraham was watching Sodom in flames. "So there were not even ten good people living in Sodom," sighed Abraham.

Sarah and Abraham had to wait a long time before a son was born to them. The parents were so happy. But Hagar became very jealous of the new baby.

Then young Ishmael began to make fun of the baby. This was too much for Sarah. One day when Ishmael was being very unpleasant she spoke to Abraham.

"Hagar and Ishmael must go away," she said. This made Abraham very sad. How could he cast out Hagar and his elder son?

Then God spoke to Abraham again. "You must let them go, Abraham," said God. "I will give Ishmael my blessing and I promise that Ishmael will one day head a great nation."

Abraham obeyed God and wept as Hagar and Ishmael went away.

But one day Ishmael would return.

Abraham's Second Son

Abraham and Sarah called their son Isaac which means 'to laugh' because they had been so happy when he was born. When Isaac was a young man God wanted to know if Abraham was still faithful to Him. So one day He told Abraham he must end his son's life. Abraham was broken-hearted but even so he was ready to obey God. God was pleased with Abraham and told him that Isaac was not to be harmed.

One day Abraham called a faithful servant to him.

"It is time for Isaac to marry," Abraham told his servant, Eliezer, who had worked for him for many years. "I know of no woman who would be a good and suitable wife for him and I would like you to find one."

In those days it was usual for a father to decide whom his children should marry. As well as a loyal servant, Abraham knew that Eliezer was a very wise man. Eliezer set out and after travelling many miles came to a well.

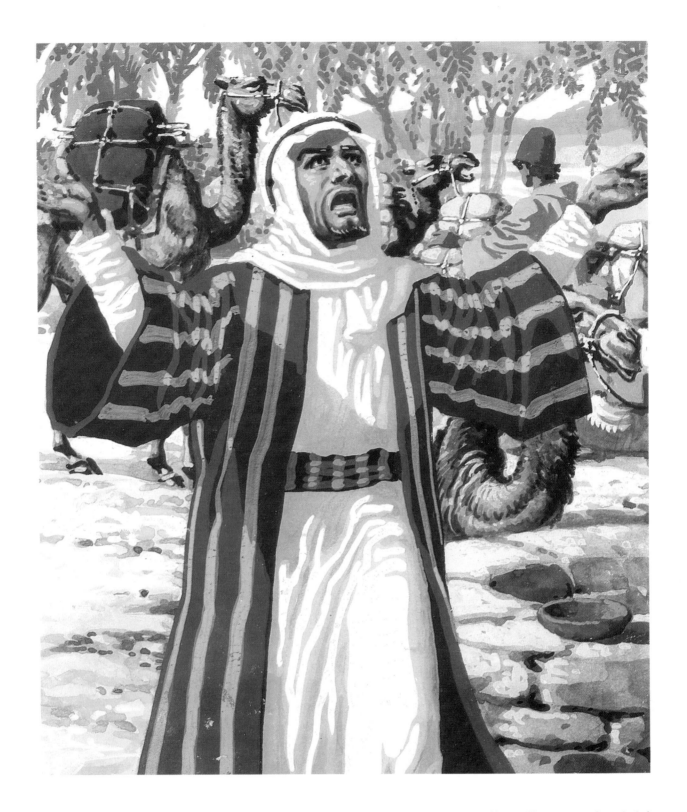

There were several lovely, young women at the well. Eliezer raised his arms and prayed to God. "O Lord, please help me to choose a wife for Isaac. I will ask each of those young women for a drink of water. Should one say to me, 'Drink, and I will give water to your camels also,' I will know that she is the one you have chosen to be Isaac's bride."

Eliezer was not to know that the first maid he spoke to was the granddaughter of Nahor who was Abraham's brother. When Eliezer asked her for a drink she smiled. "Of course," she replied, "and I will draw more water from the well for your camels." Eliezer knew then that this girl was God's chosen bride for Isaac.

Eliezer watched the young woman as she drew water from the well for his camels. Then he asked her for her name. "Rebekah," she said. Then Eliezer told her who he was and why he had spoken to her. "God has chosen you to be the wife of my master's son," he said. "Please take me to your father." Rebekah was amazed but led Eliezer to her home. He waited outside while she spoke to her father.

When Rebekah had told her mother and father and her brother, Laban, about Eliezer and what he had said, they made him welcome. "For your master, Abraham, is my uncle," smiled Bethuel, Rebekah's father. Eliezer then laid out before them the treasures that Abraham had given him to present to the young woman he had chosen to marry Isaac. "All these are yours," Eliezer said to Rebekah. The whole family could scarcely believe their eyes and ears.

"I know that my master and his son will be waiting for my return even now," said Eliezer. "Will you come with me, Rebekah?" "I will," she replied softly. The next day they set out. At last they reached Abraham's home.

Isaac had seen them from afar. He and Rebekah fell in love and married shortly afterwards.

Esau and Jacob

Many years passed and Abraham's life came to its end. At once Isaac, who was a kind man, sent for his half-brother, Ishmael, who lived not far away. Ishmael arrived and together the half-brothers went to the funeral. Then Ishmael went back home. Another twenty years passed and at last Rebekah had twin sons. How happy she and Isaac were.

The elder twin was named Esau and the younger, Jacob. As they grew up, Jacob began to dislike his brother.

Esau, meanwhile, became fond of hunting.

One day, when Esau came back from hunting he saw Jacob cooking some stew. "I am so hungry," said Esau. "May I have some of that stew?"

But Jacob said, "No, this stew is mine. You cannot have any."

Esau begged his brother to give him some food. "For I have been out hunting for two days and have had nothing to eat," he said. But Jacob said, "Esau, because you are the elder, one day what Father owns will be yours. That is your birthright. Give your birthright to me now and you can eat as much as you like." Esau was so faint with hunger he agreed. His birthright now belonged to Jacob.

As the years went by Isaac became blind. One day he called to Esau. "Take your bow and arrows and hunt for a deer," he said. "I would like to eat deer meat for dinner tonight."

Always happy to please his father, Esau hurried away. Rebekah had heard Isaac's words. It was the moment for which she had been waiting.

For a long time now she had been hoping to find a way by which Jacob could receive Isaac's blessing. In those days a father's blessing was of great importance because he gave only one and that was usually to the eldest son.

Jacob was Rebekah's second-born and her favourite.

She wanted him and not Esau, her first-born, to have the blessing. She called Jacob to her and covered his neck and hands with goatskins. Then she handed Jacob a dish of hot deer's meat and told him to take it to his father.

As soon as Jacob spoke, Isaac was puzzled. "You sound more like Jacob than Esau," he said. He ran his hand over the goatskins covering Jacob's hands and neck. "You must be Esau," he smiled, "for Jacob does not have such hairy arms and neck." Then he thanked Jacob for the deer's meat and ate it. He was so pleased he then said, "And now, my son, I will give you my blessing." This he did and Jacob thanked him and hurried away.

A few hours later Esau brought his father a dish of boiled deer's meat.

"Here is the deer's meat you asked for, Father," said Esau. "I am sorry I took so long." Isaac knew then that it was Jacob who had given him the meat and sadly he told Esau.

At first Esau was extremely angry but then he fell and wept on his father's knee. "Jacob now has my birthright and your blessing. Why has he done this to me, Father? I have never harmed him."

"Because he has always been jealous of you, my son," replied Isaac.

From then on there was nothing but hatred between the two brothers. They often quarrelled and Rebekah began to fear for Jacob's safety. She arranged for him to go and stay with her brother, Laban, who lived far away. Jacob came to say goodbye to his father.

Esau was far from sorry to see his brother leave. Rebekah never saw Jacob again.

Not long after, Esau left home, too. He went to the land of Edom, where he married Ishmael's daughter and became a great chieftain.

One night during the long journey to his uncle Laban's home, Jacob lay down to sleep. He used a stone as a pillow. He dreamed he saw a stairway on which stood many angels. The stairway reached to heaven. Then it seemed as though Jacob heard God speak. "The land on which you lie, Jacob, I will give to you and all your children. In you and them shall all the families of the world be blessed."

Laban Tricks Jacob

When Jacob awoke he was pleased. It seemed as though God had forgiven him for having stolen Esau's blessing and birthright. "Perhaps some day Esau and I can become friends again," thought Jacob. He went on his way.

Nearing Laban's home he saw many herds of cattle, flocks of sheep and many servants belonging to Laban.

Jacob was welcomed by his uncle and his uncle's two daughters, Leah, the elder, and Rachel. Jacob immediately fell in love with Rachel. After a few weeks he asked Laban if he could marry her. Laban told him that it was usual for a young man to bring gifts to the father of the girl he wished to marry. As Jacob had no money to buy gifts, Laban suggested that, instead of gifts, Jacob should work for him for seven years for nothing. Then he could marry Rachel.

Both Leah and Rachel were pleased when they heard Jacob agree for, in truth, they both loved the young man.

So Jacob worked for seven years.

Then he received a shock. Laban told him that a younger daughter could only marry after her elder sister had married so Leah would have to marry before Rachel could. Laban suggested that perhaps Jacob would like to marry Leah. If he did, he could then work another seven years for nothing and marry Rachel. Jacob liked Leah and loved Rachel.

After much thought he decided to marry Leah although he was very angry at the way he had been tricked.

In the following years Jacob had ten sons. Then he married Rachel.

After having worked for fourteen years without earning any money, Jacob decided to make up for lost time. For the next six years he worked very hard and made a lot of money. He looked after his cattle and flocks of sheep and they grew large. Now he wanted to return to his own home.

He knew that Laban would be angry if he did so. So one dark night he and his family, with all their belongings, sheep and cattle, departed while Laban was asleep. A long journey lay ahead.

Several nights later they were crossing over a brook called Jabbok when Jacob heard his name called and a stranger stepped out of the darkness. "Come with me. I have something important to say to you," he said.

Somehow Jacob felt forced to follow the stranger into the darkness. "First I wish to wrestle with you, Jacob," said the strange man as he took off his clothes. Again, Jacob felt he had to do what he was told. The two men wrestled for a long time. Then the stranger struck the inside of Jacob's thigh. As he did so, Jacob's leg gave way under him. The stranger stared down at him. "Jacob," said he, "in future you shall be known as Israel, 'The Soldier of God'." Then raising his hand, he blessed Jacob and vanished. Now Jacob understood who the stranger was. It was God.

Jacob named the place where he and God had fought 'Penial' which meant 'The Face of God'.

Then Jacob returned to his family but as he walked he began to limp and was lame for the rest of his life.

Just ahead lay the land of Edom where Esau lived. Wishing to be friends with Esau more than ever, Jacob sent ahead of him all his herdsmen, shepherds and animals as a gift to Esau.

Jacob followed with his wives and children. Some time later there came in sight an army of warriors. At their head rode a man on a horse. Even at that distance and after so many years, Jacob recognised his brother. Would Esau be a friend or a foe Jacob wondered as he dismounted and limped towards his brother. Immediately Esau threw himself from his horse and ran forward. He was laughing happily for he had forgiven his brother.

The two brothers threw their arms around each other. They were friends for evermore. "Jacob," said Esau, "I will not accept your splendid gifts. I am a rich man now and have plenty of servants and cattle and sheep of my own."

But Jacob insisted that Esau should accept. "Then you will be richer than ever," he laughed.

The End of Isaac

Esau told Jacob that although their father was still living, their mother, Rebekah, had died. Jacob was very sad to hear this because he had loved his mother dearly. Then the two brothers parted for the time being.

Later, in a small village, God appeared to Jacob again. He told him to return to Penial and there build an altar for Him. Jacob knew that his wives and his followers had been worshipping false idols. He told them that they had to give them up. Then he returned to Penial.

At Penial Jacob prayed to God and as he did so God spoke to him yet again and reminded him that from then on his name was to be Israel. God also told Jacob that he would be the father of a great nation and that his descendants would be kings. "The land which I gave to Abraham and Isaac, I now give to you," God said. Then Jacob returned to the place where, long ago on his way to Laban's home, he had dreamed of God.

There he built another altar and poured an offering on it. Now it was time to visit Isaac, his father.

Jacob and Rachel had a son named Joseph. Now, on the way to see Isaac, Rachel gave birth to another boy and he was called Benjamin. Shortly afterwards, Rachel died but Jacob's sorrow was to grow even greater. Arriving at his old home, he found that Isaac was dying. Together Jacob, now Israel, and his brother, Esau, buried their father who had lived to a great age.

The Slave Joseph

Israel and his family lived in Canaan. A great ruler, known as the Pharaoh, reigned over the nearby land of Egypt. He had a mighty army and many thousands of slaves.

Israel's two youngest sons were Joseph, for whom Israel had made a coat of many colours, and Benjamin whose name meant 'The Fortunate One'. Happily the two brothers were close friends.

Their ten brothers, the sons of Leah, hated them. It started when Joseph received the coat of many colours from his father. Their hatred increased when, several years later, Joseph told his ten brothers of a dream he had in which their sheaves of wheat bowed down to his. The brothers thought that meant Joseph considered himself to be better than they were.

In the end their hatred grew so fierce that they decided to do away with Joseph. The opportunity came when they were out guarding the family's flocks of sheep and their father sent Joseph to make sure they were looking after the sheep properly. Joseph was wearing the splendid coat which his father had given him. It had long sleeves and was striped in many colours.

As soon as Joseph appeared, his brothers sprang on him and bound him and threw him in a pit. Then, when they saw some merchants passing, they sold Joseph as a slave instead of killing him. Joseph told the merchants that he was not a slave but they only laughed at him.

The brothers then dipped Joseph's coat of many colours, which they had taken from him, in some goat's blood. They returned with it to their father and said that they had found it. Israel recognised his son's coat and thought a wild beast had killed him and he grieved for his son.

The merchants who had bought Joseph travelled to Egypt where Potiphar, a captain of Pharaoh's guard, bought him.

Joseph worked hard and well for Potiphar and found favour. At last the day came when Potiphar went out to where Joseph was working and told him that he was making him overseer of all his property.

Potiphar's wife and her hand-maiden were watching.

All went well for Joseph for a time. His master liked him and showed him great favours. The wife of Potiphar, though, was jealous and quarrelled with Joseph. She started to tell Potiphar lies about him and Potiphar began to believe her. His wife told him still more lies about Joseph until one day Potiphar did believe her and decided the only thing he could do to teach Joseph a lesson was to put him in prison. In prison with Joseph were the Pharaoh's baker and butler. Joseph was told to guard them. One night the baker and the butler had dreams that worried them.

When Joseph visited them he asked why they were sad and they told him. "Tell me your dreams," said Joseph. "I dreamed that I was carrying three baskets of good things for Pharaoh," said the baker, "but the birds flew down and ate everything in the baskets."

Then the butler told Joseph his dream. "I saw a vine with three branches. They bore grapes and I picked them and squeezed the juice into Pharaoh's cup and gave it to Pharaoh." Joseph understood the meaning of dreams and he thought for a while. He told the baker that in three days he would die. But to the butler Joseph said that in three days he would be serving Pharaoh again. So it happened. The butler was freed while the baker was put to death. As for Joseph, he remained in prison for another two years.

Pharaoh was worried one morning as he gazed out on his people in the city. He had had two dreams which he could not understand. He told his butler of his dreams and the butler said, "There is a man in prison, called Joseph, who interprets dreams." So Joseph came to Pharaoh who told him the dreams. "In the first, seven fat cows and seven thin cows came out of a river. Then the thin cows ate the fat cows," Pharaoh said. "In the second dream, seven fat ears of corn and seven thin ears grew on one stalk. The seven thin ears then ate the seven fat ears."

Joseph said, "Your dreams mean that seven years of plenty will be followed by seven years of famine."

Joseph went on, "You must appoint officers and, in the years of plenty, corn must be stored in the city so that during the famine your people will not go hungry."

"You are wise," Pharaoh told Joseph, "and I need a wise man now. If what you say comes true I must protect my people." Then he astonished Joseph. "From today, under me, you will be the most important man in Egypt."

So Joseph was made ruler of Egypt under Pharaoh. He became a good ruler and was very popular with the people.

Good and Bad Years

Sure enough there followed seven years of good summers. The people of Egypt were happy. Joseph packed all the storehouses with corn and other crops. Then came seven bad summers and there was famine everywhere, except in Egypt. People from other countries began to pour through the gates of Egypt's cities to buy food to take home.

Among them, one day, were Joseph's brothers. They came before Joseph. They did not know him but he knew them. He spoke to them in their own language and told them he thought they were spies. They said they were not. Then Joseph surprised them by telling them that he knew they had a younger brother back home. They were to go back and return with him.

"If your young brother tells me you are not spies I will believe him," said Joseph. "One of you must stay here while the rest go home." So one brother, named Simeon, stayed in Egypt. The others went back to Israel.

They had to tell Israel that Benjamin must return with them to Egypt. Israel was broken-hearted. He loved Benjamin and did not want to let him go in case he never saw him again. But the brothers took Benjamin just the same. Benjamin told Joseph that his brothers were not spies.

Joseph smiled and told his brothers who he was. He said that he would forgive them for having sold him into slavery and told them to go and bring Israel and their families and come and live in Egypt. This they did and so all ended happily.

Moses The Leader

Israel's sons and all their many children called themselves Israelites because God had changed Jacob's name to Israel. Years went by and the Israelites grew in number. The Egyptians became worried. Perhaps one day the Israelites would take their country from them. So they forced the Israelites into slavery.

Pharaoh then ordered every Israelite baby boy to be drowned. One Israelite woman put her child in a basket and left him hidden amongst the bulrushes where he was found by Pharaoh's daughter.

Looking around, Pharaoh's daughter saw an Israelite woman standing nearby. She thought she might be the baby's mother. ''Follow me to Pharaoh's palace,'' she said.

The woman was the baby's mother. Later, in the palace, the princess told the mother to take the little boy away and bring him back when he was older. The happy mother was only too pleased to do so.

Years later she returned with the boy, now named Moses, and he was brought up in the palace as if he were a royal prince. He left behind with his mother his younger brother, Aaron. Moses never forgot that he was an Israelite. In time he became a big, strong man.

One day he saw an Egyptian beating an Israelite. In great anger Moses attacked and killed the Egyptian. The order went out for him to be thrown into prison but he fled Egypt and lived in another country. One day God spoke to Moses from a burning bush.

"Moses! Moses!" came a strong voice. Startled though he was, Moses knew at once that he was listening to God. "I have listened to the prayers of the Israelites begging me to free them from slavery," God continued. "I have chosen you to take my people out of Egypt. Go to Pharaoh and ask him to free the Children of Israel."

Moses shook his head. Had he not run away from Egypt to escape prison? God reassured Moses that everything would be alright and said, "Take your brother, Aaron, with you. I will tell you the exact words I want him to say."

Then God gave Moses a long rod. "Take this. It will be of great help to you," God said. So Moses took the rod and went off to meet Aaron. At once Aaron promised to help Moses. So the two brothers travelled to Egypt. Aaron managed to arrange a meeting with Pharaoh. It was a new Pharaoh who did not know Moses. Aaron told Pharaoh they were messengers of God. Pharaoh laughed.

"If you are messengers from God give me proof." Aaron took God's rod from Moses and threw it to the ground. God had said that the rod would help them. At once the rod turned into a serpent. Again Pharaoh laughed and whispered to an officer beside him. The man hurried away and returned with some of Pharaoh's court magicians. They all carried short rods. Then swiftly they whisked the rods out of sight and flung down serpents in their place. Pharaoh grinned. His magicians were playing tricks. But Aaron's serpent attacked and ate all the others.

Pharaoh flew into a rage and refused to allow the Israelites to leave Egypt. Then Moses, with God's aid, brought down six terrible plagues on Egypt. Each time, Pharaoh said he would release the Israelites but then he changed his mind. Then came the seventh plague. The eldest child of every Egyptian family died. Even Pharaoh's son died. This was too much for the angry ruler. One day on the steps of his palace he told Moses to take the people of Israel out of Egypt.

"And go at once," Pharaoh ordered. The Israelites lost no time in leaving. But again Pharaoh changed his mind. He followed them with an army of horsemen and chariots.

When the Israelites reached the Red Sea Pharaoh's army was getting close. Then God told Moses to divide the sea with the rod so the Israelites could cross the sea on dry land.

The Israelites crossed in safety but behind them the waters suddenly poured over all the Egyptians, drowning them. Now God promised Moses he would lead the Israelites to a Promised Land. They found themselves in a wilderness with nothing to eat or drink. Then one morning they found the ground covered with manna, a sweet, white plant that is good to eat.

Every morning there was manna for them to eat. But what about water? God spoke to Moses. With the aid of God's rod, Moses could make water flow where there had been none. For more than forty years the Israelites were in the wilderness and Moses became an old man.

Day after day God saw that the Israelites had all they needed to eat and drink. They came at last to the land of the Amalekites who sent an army to stop the Israelites crossing their land. The Israelites made ready to fight. God told Moses to take his rod and hold up his arms until the Israelites had won. Moses's brother, Aaron, and another Israelite held up Moses's arms for a long time. At the end of the day the Israelites won. The Amalekites were driven away.

The Israelites thanked God for their great victory. On they went, deeper into the wilderness. It became clear that the Israelites needed laws by which to live. God told Moses to meet Him on the top of Mount Sinai nearby. He said He would give Moses the commandments which the Israelites should keep. So Moses went to the top of the mountain. He was gone for many days. The Israelites became tired of waiting for him. They spoke to Aaron.

"Moses has left us forever," they said. "Make us a god that we can worship." They kept on saying this until Aaron gave in. "Bring your gold ornaments," he said. "I will do as you ask." The people brought all their gold to him. He melted it down and cast a calf from the molten gold. The people were delighted. They set the golden calf on high and worshipped it. God was very angry.

God gave to Moses the laws by which the Israelites should live. At last Moses came down from the mountain. He found the people dancing and singing and worshipping the golden calf. He was carrying two tablets of stone on which were carved God's commandments. Moses flew into a terrible rage and flung the tablets to the ground where they broke. Then, in his fury, he smashed the golden calf.

Then Moses asked God to forgive the Israelites for being so stupid. God told Moses to meet Him on Mount Sinai for a second time. "Bring two tablets of stone like the other two and I will write my commandments on them," said God. Forty days later Moses came down from Mount Sinai carrying two new tablets on which were carved ten commandments. The first commandment was 'You shall have no other God but me'. The face of Moses shone brightly with the Glory of God.

God ordered the Israelites to build a temple in which they were to worship Him. As they had no land of their own they had to build a temple that could be easily taken down and set up anywhere. They set to work and Moses drew plans showing them what they should do. The Israelites worked long and hard to build the temple. How proud they were when at last it was finished.

Then they noticed that the temple was covered with a cloud. The cloud was a sign of God's pleasure. Moses went into the temple to pray. Afterwards the temple was taken down and its various pieces packed so that they could be carried wherever the Israelites travelled. The tablets on which the ten commandments were carved were placed in a huge portable box called the Ark. The Israelites continued their journey and always the cloud moved ahead of them, a constant sign that God was with them, as they marched. At night it changed to fire. God was watching over them and leading them towards the Promised Land.

Samson the Mighty

For forty years the Israelites wandered in the wilderness before reaching the Promised Land. Here they settled down to live in peace. To the west of them there lived a warlike tribe called the Philistines. The Philistines conquered Israel.

Then one day, a certain very strong and powerful Israelite named Samson killed a lion with his bare hands.

Before Samson was born, an angel of God visited his mother and father. "Soon you will have a son," said the angel. "He must never cut his hair nor drink wine. This will show that he is a servant of God. He will save the Israelites from the Philistines." Samson became the strongest of all the Israelites. One day he was captured by several Philistines who tied his hands together. Samson broke the rope and then fought the Philistines with the jawbone of an ass.

His fighting was so fierce that the Philistines ran away. After this battle the Israelites were so proud of Samson they made him one of their rulers. Some time later, when Samson was staying in the city of Gaza, a band of Philistines locked and bolted the big gates and waited. "When Samson tries to leave in the morning we will capture him," they thought. But that night mighty Samson tore down the gates and carried them away on his back. The Philistine watchmen did not dare stop him.

Samson fell in love with a Philistine woman whose name was Delilah. The Philistine rulers asked Delilah to find out the secret of Samson's strength. When she asked him he laughed and told her that if he were to be tied up by bowstrings or ropes that had never been used before, he would lose his strength.

So bowstrings were tied round Samson. He broke free. Then he was tied with new ropes but he broke free again.

Delilah kept on smiling and asking Samson to tell her the secret of his strength. At last he told her, "If my hair is cut, I will lose my strength." Delilah told the Philistines and one night, while Samson was asleep, Delilah had a man shave off his hair. When he awoke next morning, the Philistines were waiting. Samson tried to fight but his strength was gone. His enemies took him and put him in prison. Then they put out his eyes so that he could see no more.

Of course Samson's hair grew long again but the Philistines did not notice this. One day when thousands of people were gathered and making merry, Samson was brought out of prison so that they could mock him.

Samson was standing between two pillars. His hands touched the pillars and he called on God to give him strength. His strength returned and he pushed on the pillars. They cracked, then broke and the walls of the building fell. All the people, as well as Samson, were killed. He had taken a terrible revenge on his enemies.

Ruth

In the country of Moab, there lived a sad woman named Naomi. She was sad because her husband and both her sons had died. She lived with her two daughters-in-law named Ruth and Orpah. Naomi had once lived in Bethlehem and she wanted to return there. Ruth and Orpah had always lived in Moab so Naomi bade them both farewell. But Ruth did not want to say goodbye to her mother-in-law for she loved her very much. "Where you go, I will go. Where you live, I will live. Your people shall be my people and your God, my God," she told Naomi.

So Naomi and Ruth both set out for Bethlehem. Orpah remained in Moab. It was many miles to Bethlehem but after several weeks they arrived safely. It was harvest time and Ruth said she would like to go and glean after the reapers. Gleaners picked up the corn left by the reapers. Naomi

saw that Ruth had made up her mind so she agreed. Ruth found her way to a field which belonged to a rich man named Boaz. When Boaz saw Ruth, he fell in love with her at once. He told his workers to help Ruth gather the fallen corn.

Boaz was pleased to learn from Ruth that she was Naomi's daughter-in-law because he was a relative of Naomi. Ruth grew to love the kind man and one day they were married. They had a son whom they called Obed. His grandson was David who became King of Israel.

Samuel the Judge

In the days of Samson the High Priest of Israel was called Eli. One morning he noticed a woman praying at the door of the Tabernacle, the temple in which the Ark was stored. Eli heard the woman, whose name was Hannah, praying that soon she should have a son. "May the God of Israel grant your prayer," said Eli. Hannah thanked Eli and said if she had a son she would see that he served God all his life. Sure enough, Hannah had a son. When he was old enough she took him to Eli and put him in the High Priest's care.

"Here is my son, Samuel," she said. "As long as he lives he shall be lent to the Lord." From then on Samuel lived with Eli. Samuel was a good boy, unlike Eli's two sons who were wicked and good for nothing. Late one night Samuel was awakened by a voice that called "Samuel!" The boy thought that Eli had called. So he went and awakened Eli. But Eli said that he had not called Samuel. This happened twice more. Then Eli said, "It must be God who calls." So Eli told Samuel to return to his bed and say, "Speak, Lord, I am listening." Samuel heard the voice again and God spoke to him. He said that Eli's two sons were to die soon. Eli made Samuel tell him what God had said. "Alas, it is the will of the Lord," he said. Soon afterwards the Philistines sent an army to attack Israel.

A great battle was fought and the Israelites were heavily defeated. Four thousand of them were slain. The survivors fled to the High Priest. "We must gather together another army," they said, "and fight the Philistines again. This time we must take the Ark with us. Then God will be on our side and we will defeat our enemies." So the Israelites went out to meet the Philistines again.

Once more they were defeated and Eli's two sons died in the battle. God's words to Samuel had come true. One Israelite escaped from the raging battle and ran to tell the High Priest what had happened. When Eli heard that his sons were dead, he fell to the ground and died too.

So the Ark fell into the hands of the Philistines but wherever they took it, it brought sickness and death to everybody living nearby. Finally the Ark was safely returned to the Israelites.

Samuel lived on and became one of Israel's Judges. He was now a very important man in Israel.

Saul and David

God spoke to Samuel one day and said, "Tomorrow I will send you a man from the Benjamite tribe. You must make him captain of the Israelites so that he may lead them against their enemies." The next day, there came to Samuel a very tall, handsome man named Saul. He was a farmer's son who was searching for some lost asses. He thought that Samuel, who was known to be very clever and could speak with God, might tell him where he could find his animals. Samuel told him to forget his asses and a few days later Samuel had Saul crowned King of Israel.

Saul was crowned in the town of Mizpeh where Samuel had told the people of Israel to come and greet their new and first King. When Samuel told them that God had chosen Saul, the son of a farmer, to be king, a great cheer went up.

The Ammonites were then at war with Israel and were attacking the city of Jabesh-Gilead. Their army surrounded the beautiful city.

Bravely, Saul led an Israelite army against the Ammonites and defeated them before they could take the city.

During the years that followed, the Israelites fought battles against many people. But when Israel's old enemies, the Philistines, rode out to attack them, Saul always led his army to victory.

Saul did not always do what God wanted him to and this made God angry. Because of this Samuel had to tell Saul that God had chosen a new king for the Israelites.

At about this time a young shepherd named David slew a lion that was killing his sheep.

God spoke to Samuel again. "Go to Bethlehem and call on a man named Jesse. One of his sons is to be King of Israel." Samuel went to Bethlehem.

Jesse had eight sons. Samuel met them one by one. Silence followed. Then Samuel asked Jesse if he had any more sons. "My youngest," replied Jesse. "He minds my sheep." Samuel heard God's voice again. "Anoint that boy," He said and this Samuel obeyed.

How puzzled Jesse must have been when the famous Samuel anointed young David. Samuel returned to Saul's palace but said nothing. Now King Saul was a strange man who often fell into rages. His mind never seemed to be at peace. One day a servant said to him, "I know a young shepherd in Bethlehem who can play the harp better than anyone else. His music will soothe your troubled mind." Saul sent for the shepherd. It was David and David often played for Saul.

Once again the Philistines declared war on Israel. They sent another huge army. With them this time came a giant of a man named Goliath. Saul called the men of Israel to arms. David's seven brothers joined the army. Hearing this David took food and wine to his brothers. He was with them when Goliath suddenly strode towards them with only one Philistine warrior. "If you have a man strong enough to fight with me and beat me, we shall surrender to you. If I win, you shall surrender to us," shouted Goliath.

King Saul told his soldiers that if any man could kill Goliath he would make him rich and give him one of his daughters in marriage. Not one man stepped forward. Then David spoke, "I will fight Goliath," he said. Saul offered him his own armour but David said, "No. God helped me to fight lions and bears to protect my father's sheep. I know He will help me to fight Goliath, too." David took only his sling and a few stones. He put one stone in his sling and aimed it at Goliath. The stone struck Goliath's forehead and the big man fell.

In an instant David sped forward and taking Goliath's own sword, slew the giant. The whole Israelite army cheered David. Angrily the Philistines accepted Goliath's defeat and surrendered their army to King Saul. Even though Saul was grateful to David, he hated the idea that a poor, young man should marry one of his daughters. Then, one day, he quarrelled with David. While he was playing his harp, Saul flung a spear at him.

David fled from Saul's anger. Later the king's temper died down but his feelings towards David were the same. He thought David had been lucky to slay Goliath. Now he did not wish to make David rich as he had promised. "And neither shall he marry one of my daughters," declared Saul. However, he pretended that he was still friendly towards David. "I can see you are a brave soldier," he told him.

"You can marry one of my daughters but only after you have defeated the Philistines in another battle."

So David led out an Israelite army which defeated the Philistines. Saul then allowed David to marry his daughter, Michal. One night David learned that Saul was planning to have him killed. Michal helped David fix a rope to a window opening and slide down to safety. By the time Saul's soldiers broke into the house, David was far away.

Saul's son, Jonathan, tried to make peace between his father and David. Saul refused to listen. So Jonathan had to tell David never to return to the king's court.

David gathered round him many brave men who had also turned against Saul for various reasons. Then Saul tried to capture David.

David acted. One night when Saul was sleeping in a cave, David entered quietly and slashed Saul's robe to let him know he had been there. On another occasion when the king was sleeping amongst his soldiers, David crept through them and took the king's spear from his side. Saul now knew that twice David could have killed him.

The Philistines had never given up hope of conquering the Israelites. They rose once again and Saul, with his son, Jonathan, rode out to meet them. This time the Israelites were defeated and Jonathan was killed. Saul, badly wounded and not wanting to fall into the hands of his enemy, killed himself with his own sword.

The people now turned towards David who swore to avenge the Israelites' defeat. He led another army to victory over their old enemy and became the second and greatest King of Israel.

Jonah and the Whale

New enemies, the Assyrians, swore to destroy Israel. They sent a mighty army, defeated the Israelites and broke them up into tribes. One tribe settled in Judah where lived a man of God called Jonah. One day, God told Jonah to go to the Assyrian city of Nineveh and tell them that their wickedness had angered Him. Jonah did not want to do this so he went aboard a ship headed in the other direction. A storm blew up and, to help the ship through the storm, the seamen threw overboard all that was not necessary. Jonah told them to throw him overboard and the sea would calm down. They

did and he was swallowed by a whale. Three days later he was flung out of the whale's mouth on to dry land. Jonah was back in Judah. Jonah, knowing that God had caused the storm, went to Nineveh and told the people what God had said. In fear, the Assyrians decided to live good lives and God forgave their wickedness. Jonah, too, had pleased God.

Daniel and his Friends

Time and time again other tribes and nations became jealous of the people of Israel. Their God, it seemed, was always taking care of them. How else could the Israelites defeat their enemies, one by one. Then one day, terrible news was brought to the city of Jerusalem. The army of the King of Babylon was on its way to capture the city.

Even as the people of Jerusalem ran to arm themselves, the warriors of Babylon were attacking farmers on the outskirts of the city. There was no time for the people of Jerusalem to protect themselves. The city was captured and many citizens were taken back to Babylon as prisoners. Among them were four young princes named Daniel, Shadrach, Meshach and Abednego. Because they were princes they were brought before Nebuchadnezzar who was the King of Babylon.

It became clear to the king that the four princes were clever and that Daniel could tell him the meaning of his dreams. Nebuchadnezzar came to rely on Daniel and his three friends.

At last Daniel was made chief over all the king's wise men at court.

Many years went by. The king worshipped his own god and had a gigantic golden statue of this god built in the plain of Dura.

This statue shone brilliantly in the sunlight. The king ordered everyone in his kingdom to worship it.

Daniel was away at the time but Shadrach, Meshach and Abednego refused to worship any other god but their own.

This made Nebuchadnezzar angry. He raged at them, "Obey me or I will have you flung into a furnace of fire." Again they refused. So the king had them bound and thrown into the fire. The flames were so fierce that the men who threw them into the fire were burnt to death. Then Nebuchadnezzar thought he saw Shadrach, Meshach and Abednego standing together in the middle of the roaring flames.

Then the king thought he saw another figure standing with the three friends. "It must be their God," he said. He called to the three, and as they walked from the fire, unburnt, he said that nobody was ever to insult their God.

Nebuchadnezzar died. The next king was an evil man named Belshazzar. He was seated at a feast one day when a phantom hand appeared and wrote MENE MENE TEKEL UPHARSIN on the wall. Daniel was sent for and asked its meaning. "If you can tell me, I will make you rich," said the king. But he gasped in terror when Daniel said the words meant that God had weighed Belshazzar in the balance and found him wanting. In other words, God thought that Belshazzar was lacking in goodness and was wicked.

That God meant this was later proved when Babylon was invaded by the Persians and Belshazzar was killed. Darius, the Persian King, then became the ruler of Babylon.

He ruled with the help of three governors. Chief of these was Daniel. One day, the king decreed that for thirty days only he, the king, could ask for help from any god. Anyone who disobeyed would be thrown to the lions. Daniel disobeyed and was put in the lions' den. Amazingly the lions did not attack him. The next day he was freed. ''Daniel's God has saved him,'' said the king.

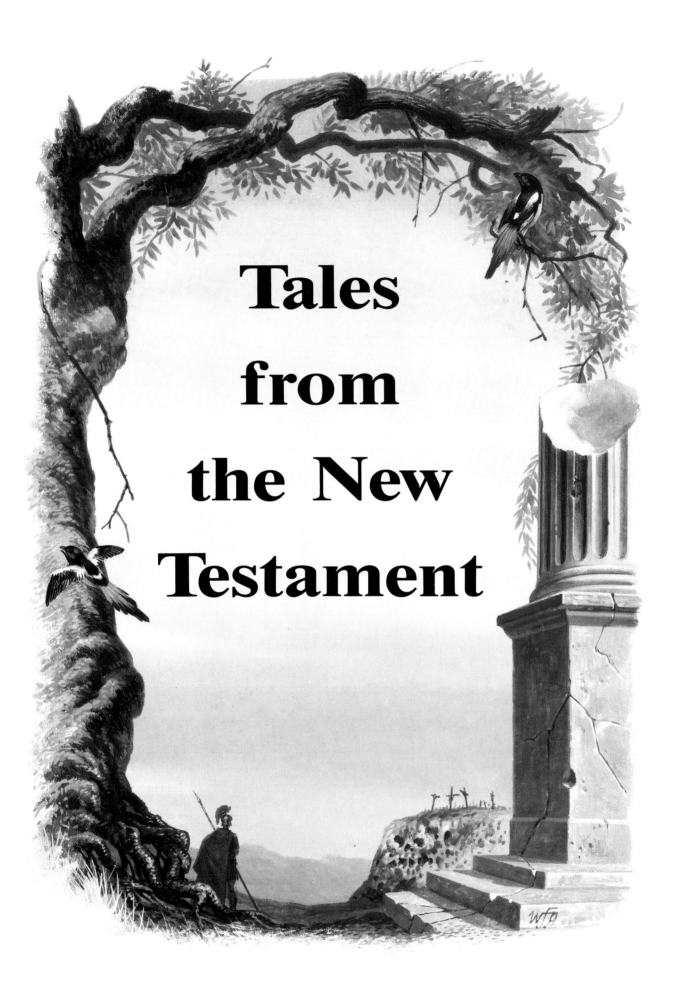

Tales

from

the New

Testament

Jesus Is Born

Two thousand years ago the Holy Land was part of the mighty Roman Empire which taxed all its people. Everyone had to go the place where they were born to be taxed.

One night a man named Joseph, together with his wife, Mary, arrived in Bethlehem. He was from Nazareth and had come to pay his taxes. He knocked on the door of an inn because he needed a room for the night. Mary was expecting her baby. The innkeeper told Joseph that the inn was full. All he could offer them was his stable. That night, with a bright star shining overhead, Mary's baby son was born. Mary wrapped him up warmly and laid him in a manger.

That night shepherds came to the stable. They said that an angel had told them that this day a Saviour would be born and would be found lying in a manger. They saw the baby Jesus and left to spread the news of the angel's message.

When Jesus was born, the name of the king was Herod, and three wise men from the east went to see him. "Where is the babe who is born to be King of the Jews?" they asked Herod. "We have followed his star and come to worship him." Herod sent them to Bethlehem and asked them to search for the child and to tell him where the baby was so that he, too, could worship him.

The three wise men set off for Bethlehem and at last reached the place where Mary and Joseph were with the baby Jesus. When they saw the child they bowed down and worshipped him and gave him gifts of gold, frankincense and myrrh.

Then they departed. But they did not go back to Herod because, that night in a dream, God forbade them to do so. They stole away secretly and travelled a different route home to escape any pursuers that Herod might send after them.

King Herod, who was a cruel man, then gave orders that every boy under the age of two who was living in Bethlehem should be slain. The Lord warned Joseph of this and the Holy Family left Bethlehem at once.

Joseph, Mary and the baby Jesus escaped the soldiers who were hunting all the little boys in Bethlehem. Joseph took his wife and child to Egypt and stayed there several years. King Herod died and Joseph decided to return to Nazareth where he had lived. Joseph was a carpenter so he opened a carpenter's shop. At times the boy Jesus helped him. Then, one day, Jesus, who was now twelve years old, went missing. Joseph and Mary searched everywhere for him. They found him, at last, in the Temple sitting with the religious teachers, listening to them and asking questions. Jesus astonished the teachers with his learning. His parents took him home. "Why did you do this?" they asked. Jesus looked surprised. "Do you not understand that I was about my Father's business?" he said. By "Father" Jesus meant God. His parents were astonished at this reply.

The Man Jesus

Jesus was a man when he heard about a strange wanderer called John the Baptist. John never cut his hair, drank only water and ate very little. He always spoke of duty to God and told his listeners that they should repent any wickedness. Those who repented he would baptise in the River Jordan. Jesus decided that he would leave home and be baptised by John. When John saw Jesus coming he said, ''Why have you come to me when you should be baptising me?'' Somehow John knew who Jesus was.

Jesus shook his head. "No," he said to John. "You must baptise me."
As John baptised Jesus the voice of God was heard speaking to Jesus, "You
are my beloved son. I am well pleased with you."

Mary and Jesus were later asked to a wedding feast in the town of Cana.
After a while Mary came and said to Jesus, "All the wine has been drunk.
There is none left." Jesus quietly turned many jugs of water into wine. This
was the first miracle.

People everywhere in Cana spoke about this wonderful event. Jesus moved to the town of Capernaum. A nobleman, who had a son lying ill at home, came and threw himself down before Jesus. He begged Jesus to save his son who was dying. "Go on your way. Your son lives," said Jesus gently. The nobleman believed the words of Jesus and went on his way. Along the road a servant met him and said, "Your son lives." The father asked when his son had begun to get better. When they told him, the father knew that his son's recovery started at the time Jesus had spoken to him.

Walking one day beside a pool known as Bethesda, Jesus saw a man who had been ill for thirty-eight years. People came to the pool which, at certain times of the year, contained water that cured them. "Do you want to be well?" Jesus asked the man. "Yes, but I cannot walk and there is nobody here to help me into the pool." "Rise, take up your bed and walk," said Jesus. Immediately the man was well. He rose up, rolled up his mat and walked away. Jesus went on his way smiling.

Jesus came to the sea of Galilee. Many people had followed him. There he saw some fishermen who had been fishing all night without catching any fish. He asked two of them, named Simon Peter and Andrew, to row him a little way out to sea. The fishermen took Jesus in their boat and rowed him a little way from shore.

Then Jesus started to speak and his voice carried to the people on the shore. They all listened carefully to this wandering stranger who told them that God expected everyone to try to lead good lives. They listened to everything he had to say. They asked questions and always Jesus had a ready answer. Then he asked Andrew and Simon Peter, who was better known as just Peter, to row him back to shore. "Before you do," he said, "cast out your nets." "It is no use," said Andrew. "We have been out fishing all night and caught nothing."

"Even so," said Jesus, "do as I say." So Andrew and Peter threw out their nets, although they thought the fish had left that part of the sea. To their astonishment, when they tried to pull in their nets they were too heavy and they asked two other fishermen, named James and John, to come and help them. Even with four people, the nets were so full of fish that they broke. Later, Jesus spoke to all the fishermen and reminded them to lead good lives. To Andrew and Peter he said, looking deeply into their eyes, "Follow me and I will make you fishers of men." They nodded and followed him. By 'fishers of men' Jesus meant that he wanted them to go with him and help teach the people how to lead good lives and please God. Later, James and John, who were brothers and had helped Andrew and Peter pull in their nets, joined Jesus.

The followers of Jesus were called disciples. A few days later, Jesus and his four disciples went to Peter's house. The mother of Peter's wife was ill with a high fever. Jesus took her hand in his and at once the fever left her.

That evening many sick people, who had heard where Jesus was, came to Peter's house. They begged Jesus to cure them. He laid his hands on all those who were ill and healed them.

A month later, Jesus came upon a party of ten people suffering from leprosy. They each had to wear a bell so that healthy people, on hearing the bells, could avoid contact with them. Lepers could only mix with other people if they proved to their priest they were cured.

Jesus touched them all and all of them were cured. Nine of them hurried away to see the priest. Only one man remained behind.

The man fell on his knees before Jesus. "Thank you, Lord," he cried. Jesus gazed down at him sadly. "Did I not cure ten of you?" he asked. "Where are the other nine?" The man shook his head. Jesus gently raised the man to his feet. "Go your way," he said. "Your faith has made you whole." The man sped after his companions. "You should all remember that you have been cured by the power of the Son of God," he said to them angrily.

The Sermon on the Mount

Jesus moved from town to town preaching the word of God and healing people. A multitude of people always followed him. He left them one night to go up into a mountain to be alone in prayer.

In the morning, when he came down, he named his twelve disciples and to them and the multitude of people, he began to speak. "Blessed are the poor and simple people. The Kingdom of Heaven is theirs. Blessed are those who are sad. They shall be made happy."

Jesus was teaching God's thoughts to the people who were listening. "God blesses those who are gentle, those who wish to be good and those who are merciful and can forgive their enemies. Those of you who are pure in heart will understand what God is saying. Try to be peaceful. God will then call you His children."

Jesus ended with these words, "Blessed are those who are punished for believing in me." Then he gave them the Lord's prayer beginning with "Our Father who art in heaven, Hallowed be Thy name" and ending with "Thine is the kingdom, the power and the glory, for ever and ever. Amen."

Crowds followed Jesus everywhere. One day four men carried a crippled friend to a house where Jesus was preaching. It was crowded and they could not enter. So they went up to the roof, removed a lot of tiles and lowered him down through the roof to get to Jesus who could make him well.

When Jesus looked up and saw that they had faith in him, he said to the man, who had not always been good, "Your sins are forgiven."

It was in Capernaum that Jesus heard of a Roman Centurion who had helped with the building of a Jewish synagogue. A good servant of the Centurion was now sick with a serious illness called palsy. The elders of the synagogue asked Jesus if he could help.

Jesus went to the Centurion's house. But the soldier said to Jesus, "I am not good enough for you to enter my house. Only say the word and my servant will be healed."

"Because you believe in the true God, your servant is already better," said Jesus. The Centurion's faith had saved his servant's life. A week later, in the town of Nain, Jesus saw the body of a boy being carried by on a stretcher. His weeping mother was a widow. Jesus took pity on her saying, "Weep not." He touched the stretcher and the bearers stood still. Then said Jesus, "Young man, I say unto you, arise." And the boy sat up and spoke.

One day, a blind and dumb man was brought to Jesus. Now the Jews believed that such a man was possessed by a devil and was evil. When he cured the man, some of his enemies said that the power of Jesus to cure people must have come from the Prince of Devils himself.

"Would Satan cast out Satan?" Jesus asked. "It is God who has cast out the devil that might have been in this man. If you say otherwise you are making God angry. Now I tell you this. If you are not with me, you are against me."

Jesus walked away, leaving behind him many enemies. Several of them were important in politics.

In Capernaum, that autumn, Jesus was on his way to cure the daughter of Jairus, a governor of a synagogue. As he walked, a woman who was ill touched the hem of his robe. "Lord, I believe in you," she said, trembling as she spoke. "Your faith has helped you," said Jesus. "Go in peace."

At that moment a messenger came to tell Jesus that the daughter of Jairus was dead and there was no longer any need to come. Jairus was weeping when Jesus arrived.

"Dry your eyes, Jairus. Do not be afraid, just believe," said Jesus. He sent everyone from the room, except her parents, then took the girl's hand and said to her, "I say to you, arise." The girl opened her eyes as life came back to her and she got up and walked.

Friends of Jairus, who had come to say they were sorry his daughter had died, marvelled that she was better. "Jesus has worked another miracle," they said.

Once, five thousand people gathered to listen to Jesus. He spoke and taught them and healed those who were sick. In the evening the disciples wanted the people sent away because they were hungry and needed to go back to their villages to eat.

Jesus said, "They need not go. You can feed them."

But the disciples said, "We have only five loaves and two fishes in a basket."

"Bring the basket to me," said Jesus.

Jesus looked round at the crowd. "Ask them to sit down," he said to Andrew and Peter. As soon as the people were seated, Jesus took the loaves and fishes and gave thanks. He handed them to his disciples who kept breaking them and distributing them to the people. When all had eaten as much as they wanted Jesus told the disciples to gather up what was left. Twelve baskets were filled!

Later at Bethsaida, Jesus saw a blind man. Jesus put his fingers to his mouth and wet the man's eyes. Suddenly the man said, "I see trees that look like men walking." Jesus touched his eyes again and the man saw clearly.

Jesus Walks on the Water

Jesus had many enemies and many friends. A group of people called Zealots had heard about Jesus and his wonderful cures. They wanted to make Jesus their king and wanted Jesus to lead them to fight their Roman conquerors. But Jesus refused.

He was talking to them one day on the banks of the Sea of Galilee. He had been wanting to take his disciples across the sea to speak to people who lived on the other side. He was still talking to the Zealots when night began to fall. He said to his disciples, "You go on before me. I will follow you later." So the disciples boarded a ship and set sail. Then a storm blew up. The Zealots decided to go home. They left Jesus behind gazing out to sea.

Jesus saw his disciples lowering the sails of their ship. Not all his disciples had been fishermen. Jesus knew that some would be afraid of the storm. Hours later, through the driving rain, they saw Jesus walking towards them on the water. "Be not afraid. It is I," they heard Jesus call. The disciples could scarcely believe their ears. "If it is you, Lord," shouted Peter, "help me to walk on the water, too." Jesus held out his hand and Peter walked towards him.

As Jesus led Peter safely back to the ship, the wind dropped. Reaching land, the disciples fell on their knees. "Truly, you are the Son of God," they said.

It was summertime and Jesus went back to Capernaum. One morning, several children gathered to see Jesus and his disciples tried to push them to one side. But Jesus said, "No, let the children come to me for the Kingdom of God is made up of those who are like these innocent children." Then he blessed them.

Jesus became famous everywhere and he made many friends who believed in him. But there were many others who said he was not the Son of God. "He is only the son of a carpenter," they would say. They hoped they could somehow trick him into saying something against the laws that would help them to have him arrested.

One day, they brought to Jesus a woman against whom certain charges had been made. "This woman is sinful. She should be stoned to death by Jewish law," they said. "What do you say, Jesus?" Jesus knew they wanted him to say the woman had done no wrong so that they could say he was against the law. Then he could be put to death with the woman. Quietly Jesus stopped and started to write in the dust on the floor. They kept on asking him questions. At last Jesus looked up at them. "Let him among you who is without sin cast the first stone at this woman," he said.

His enemies were ashamed and went out one by one. After they had gone, Jesus said to the woman, "Not one has condemned you. Neither do I. Go - sin no more."

The Stories Jesus Told

A lawyer once asked Jesus how he could make sure of going to heaven one day. Jesus told him to love his neighbour and God. "Who is my neighbour?" asked the lawyer. Jesus told him a story about a traveller who was set upon by thieves and robbed of all his clothes and his money. One after another three men passed the wounded man. Only one stopped to help him.

"The first passer-by was a Jewish priest," said Jesus. "The second was a Jewish minister. The third man was a Samaritan from far-off Samaria." Jesus knew that the Jews disliked Samaritans. The lawyer was a Jew. Jesus continued, "The Samaritan bathed the man's wounds, helped him on to his own beast and took him to an inn. Which of the three was the man's neighbour?" asked Jesus. "He who helped the man," said the lawyer. "Then go on your way and do likewise," Jesus told him. The lawyer went on his way, wondering.

"How often must we pray to God and ask for His help?" the disciples asked Jesus one day. "Listen," said Jesus, and he told them how, very late one night, a man was awakened by somebody knocking on his door below. He went to a window and looked out. In the street was a friend of his who said, "A friend of mine has just arrived after a long journey. He is tired and hungry. I have no food at home. Please lend me three loaves." "No," said the man upstairs. But his friend kept on knocking until the weary man came down and gave him three loaves. "So you see," ended Jesus, "every day you must say the Lord's prayer and sooner or later God will help you. It is as though you are knocking on the door of heaven."

One Sunday, Jesus went to Jerusalem. On his way he was greeted by large cheering crowds. When he arrived at the temple he became angry because the temple was full of cattle and merchants and money-changers who were cheating the people. Jesus took a whip of small cords and drove the animals and the people out of the temple. One man who was selling doves tried to argue with

Jesus. But Jesus refused to listen to him. "Be off with you," cried Jesus. "You must never make God's house a market-place." The stall-holders and merchants went at once to the elders of the church and told them that Jesus had whipped them out of the temple. "It is that trouble-maker Jesus, the carpenter's son, again," said a Chief Priest.

"We should have put an end to that man a long time ago," said an elder. "Then let us waste no more time," said another. "We will go to Caiaphas, the High Priest, and ask him to do all he can to rid us of this man. The people are beginning to think that he is more important than we are." This was agreed and they all went to speak to the High Priest.

Caiaphas was a stern man who had watched and made note of how important Jesus had now become. "There is only one way that we can put an end to this fellow who calls himself the Son of God," he said. "He must die." Now a few days later the Feast of the Passover was due to take place. This is an eight-day Jewish festival and it had been held ever since the days of Moses. Just before he and the people of Israel set out for the Promised Land, the Egyptians had angered God and one night, every first-born child in the country died except the children of the Israelites.

The Last Days of Jesus

The anger of God had passed over the heads of the Jewish children. That is why the feast is called the Passover. "We will have Jesus arrested and then put an end to his life," the elders told Caiaphas. The High Priest nodded. "But not during the Feast of the Passover," he said. "That would be wrong. We must arrest him as soon as possible." One disciple, named Judas, learned about the plot to have Jesus arrested. He knew that the elders would pay a lot of money to anyone who was prepared to betray Jesus. He went to them secretly.

Although they offered a lot of money, Judus only accepted thirty pieces of silver to help them arrest Jesus. That night Jesus and his disciples sat down to a last supper. While they ate, Jesus said to them that later he would go to the Garden of Gethsemane to pray. Then he told them that one of them would betray him. "Who?" they all asked.

Jesus shook his head. Peter said, "Lord, you know it is not I, for I would lay down my life for you." Jesus looked at Peter. "Yet," he said, "before the cock crows tomorrow morning you will have denied knowing me three times."

Then Jesus whispered to Judas, "What you have to do, do quickly." Judas realised that somehow Jesus knew about his meeting with the elders. He crept quietly from the room.

Again and again Peter said he would never deny to anyone that he knew
Jesus. But Jesus smiled gently. Then he took Peter, James and John with
him to the Garden of Gethsemane. "Stay awake and watch over me while
I pray," he said. But while Jesus prayed, his disciples fell asleep and it was
then that the Chief Priests with some Roman soldiers entered the Garden.
With them was Judas. He went to Jesus and kissed him. This was the signal
for the soldiers to arrest Jesus. The three disciples awoke. When he saw
what was happening Peter cut off the ear of one of the men.

Sternly Jesus told Peter to put up his sword. He stretched out his hand and healed the man's ear. Then the soldiers took Jesus away. During the night Peter was asked three times by various people if he knew Jesus. Each time, in fear of his life, he said, "No." On the last occasion he heard the cock crow and remembered the words of Jesus. In the morning Jesus was taken before the Jewish court called the Sanhedrin. The chief judge was Caiaphas, who tried to trick Jesus with many cunning questions.

Jesus was too clever to be trapped by Caiaphas. He remained silent until Caiaphas asked him if he was the Son of God. ''Yes,'' replied Jesus, ''and one day you will see God's son sitting on His right hand.'' It was an offence in the Jewish religion to claim to be the Son of God. Caiaphas could now condemn Jesus to death. Jesus was taken away and Caiaphas and the Chief Priests went off to speak to Pontius Pilate, the Roman Governor.

Although Jesus had been condemned to death by the Jewish court, only Pontius Pilate could order the sentence to be carried out. Caiaphas asked Pilate to give the sentence. Pilate ordered Jesus to be brought before him. Perhaps he had learned that Judas, the man who had betrayed Jesus, had killed himself. If he had, what was the reason? Had Judas betrayed an innocent man? At all events, Pontius Pilate was not in a hurry to say Jesus should die. When Jesus came before him, Pilate asked him questions. At the same time he tried to help Jesus. When he had asked his last question he told Caiaphas that he could find no fault in Jesus. "Free him," he said. But Caiaphas refused to obey.

Then Pilate said that as Jesus was a man of Galilee, it was only right that Herod, King of Galilee, should order the death of Jesus. Caiaphas could not deny this, so Jesus was taken before King Herod. But the king did not want to give the death sentence either. He sent Jesus back to Pilate.

Pilate did not want to send Jesus to his death. He now remembered that during the Passover it was usual that one condemned prisoner could be released. Pilate had sentenced to death an evil man named Barabbas. So he called together the elders and the people and said, "Choose between this good man, Jesus, and this wicked man, Barabbas. Which of them do you say should die?" Caiaphas made sure that those people who wanted Jesus dead should shout louder than the friends of Jesus. So the prison guards let Barabbas go free.

Pilate then said, "Then Jesus must die." The soldiers took Jesus. They plaited a crown of thorns and put it on him.

A guard of soldiers forced back the crowd. Jesus was then led towards a hill called Calvary. He knew that he was going to die. Two other prisoners were to die with him. All three were to be crucified. Two of the prisoners carried their own crosses but Jesus had been so ill-treated since he had been taken prisoner that he was too weak. A friend of Jesus, named Simon of Cyrene, carried the cross for him.

On the hill of Calvary Jesus and the other two prisoners were nailed to their crosses. Over the head of Jesus was fixed a notice which read 'Jesus of Nazareth, King of the Jews'. Pilate had written this notice. Then the soldiers stripped Jesus and divided his clothes. This was usually done to people who were to die. Mary, the mother of Jesus, his disciple, John, and Mary Magdalene, a woman who had been befriended by Jesus, stood nearby. One of the men on the cross beside Jesus said, "Lord, remember me when you come into your Kingdom." And Jesus replied, "Truly, I tell you, today you shall be with me in Paradise."

Then darkness fell over the land from the sixth hour until the ninth hour. Jesus said he was thirsty.

Three days later, Mary Magdalene went to the garden. The big stone had been rolled away. Mary entered the tomb and saw a young man in a long, white garment. "You are looking for Jesus of Nazareth who was crucified," he said, "but he is risen. Go now, and tell the disciples that Jesus will go to Galilee before them and they will see him there." Mary left and went and told the

disciples that Jesus had risen and that she had seen and spoken to him. But the disciples did not believe her.

Later that day, two men were walking along the road to Emmaus, a village about eight miles from Jerusalem. They were talking about what had happened to Jesus and were unhappy. A stranger joined them. It was Jesus but the men did not recognise him. "Why are you sad?" he asked. The men told Jesus all that had occurred in the last few days and Jesus then spoke to them about the scriptures. When the men reached home they invited Jesus to eat with them. When the food and wine was brought in Jesus blessed it. The men suddenly understood that Jesus was sitting with them. Then Jesus disappeared.

The men hurried back to Jerusalem to tell Peter and the other disciples. While they were speaking Jesus appeared again amongst them. At first they were frightened so Jesus said, "See and touch my hands and feet," and he spoke to them all, saying, "I am with you always, even unto the end of the world." He led them after, to the Mount of Olives. He blessed them all. A little later, a cloud seemed to part him from their sight. As the disciples and the followers of Jesus stared at the cloud, two men in white stood by them. "Jesus is taken from you into heaven," they said. "One day he will come again, just as you have seen him go into heaven." Then the two strange men vanished.